# NAVIGATING
# POTTY
# TIME

## A BEGINNERS MANUAL FOR AUTISM PARENTS

This book offers guidance and support for parents embarking on the journey of toilet training their autistic children, emphasizing patience, understanding, and tailored strategies.

## DENISE OREILLY, M.S.

# Welcome!

My name is Denise O'Reilly! Most of you probably already know me from Instagram! I am a Licensed Behavior Specialist with my Masters in Applied Behavior Analysis.

I have been a behavioral ABA therapist for over 11 years for autistic children, and I found it to be my passion! God also blessed me with a wonderful son who is also autistic. I believe God made me his mother not only because he knew I'd be the best mom for him but because he knew that I would be able to help so many others who are in the same boat as I am! My true calling is to help other parents/caregivers who don't have the resources or help available to them.

I am so excited that you are here. I put my knowledge as a therapist, as well as my personal experiences with my son, into this Book. I am here for whatever you may need! You can always schedule a consultation call, follow us on Instagram if you haven't already, and join our amazing community on "The Autism Parent" Facebook group! I wish you the best of luck on your potty training journey with your little ones, and I hope you find this Book helpful!

Denise O'Reilly

# THE AUTISM PARENT

## Accept.Learn.Thrive

# CONTENTS

# CONTENTS

# CHAPTER 1
# UNDERSTANDING ASD

# Introduction: Overview of Autism Spectrum Disorder (ASD) Characteristics

Autism spectrum disorder, commonly known as ASD, is a complex developmental disability that affects a person's ability to communicate, socialize, and interact with others. It is called a "spectrum" because how it affects individuals varies greatly, from mild to severe.

The Diagnostic and Statistical Manual of Mental Disorders, 5th edition, text revision (DSM-5-TR) outlines diagnostic criteria based on functioning in two domains:

 Social Communication

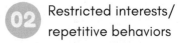 Restricted interests/ repetitive behaviors

These criteria state that autistic people sometimes benefit from support, but there's a wide range of differences in support needs.

Some autistics can have a regular conversation and communicate accurately with others. They might need some occasional help with social cues or regulating their emotions. With proper therapy, they can learn how to be social without assistance in the areas they struggle with.

Some individuals are nonspeaking and have high sensitivity to sensory input. They often communicate with emotional and behavioral outbursts mainly because they can't communicate what they want or how they feel. There are different things they can use to communicate, such as augmentative and alternative communication devices (AAC), Picture PEC cards, and even sign language to be able to communicate their wants and needs.

When diagnosing ASD, doctors assign levels of autism to help the person get the amount of support that's right for them.

A person can also have different levels across the two domains — for example, someone might have level 1 autism for social communication and level 2 for restricted/repetitive behaviors. Each of those criteria has its degree of support. (Lovering, 2022)

# THERE ARE THREE PRIMARY LEVELS OF ASD:

The DSM-5-TR classifies Autism into three levels based on the amount of support needed.

## Level 1: "Requiring Support"

Trouble understanding and finding social cues

Rigid or inflexible behavior

Some stress during transitions

May benefit from therapy and life skills coaching

At this level, individuals with Autism often face challenges in social communication that can cause noticeable impairments without support. For instance, they might need help to initiate social interactions and may display atypical or unsuccessful responses to social overtures of others. They may also need help with organization and planning, which can hamper independence. These individuals typically speak in full sentences and engage in communication but might struggle with more nuanced aspects, such as back-and-forth conversation. Therapy for level 1 restricted and repetitive behaviors can help an autistic person learn self-regulation strategies. At school, they can benefit from accommodations like extra time for tests and intermittent support from an education assistant (EA).

| Level 1: Social communication characteristics may include: | Level 1: Restricted interests and repetitive behavior traits can be: |
|---|---|
| Trouble understanding or complying with social conventions | A need for additional personal organization strategies |
| The appearance of disinterest in social interactions | Behavioral rigidity and inflexibility |
| Some emotional or sensory dysregulation | Stress during transitions |
| | Attention span differences |
| | Perseveration (focusing on something longer than is helpful) |

## Level 2: "Requiring Substantial Support"

Atypical social behavior, like walking away mid-conversation

High interest in specific topics

Noticeable distress when faced with change

May need school accommodations like reading help or social skills support

Individuals at this level face more severe challenges in social communication than those at Level 1. They might have limited speech and struggle significantly with nonverbal communicative behaviors used for social interaction. For instance, they may need help understanding and responding to social cues, making it hard to form and sustain relationships. Repetitive behaviors are more obvious and can interfere with functioning in various contexts. They might need school accommodations like scribing or reading support and an assistant nearby to help with social interactions during recess and lunch breaks. They may also have schoolwork adapted to their level and be part of a social skills group.

| Level 2: Social communication traits may include: | Level 2: Restricted interests and repetitive behavior traits can be: |
|---|---|
| Using fewer words or noticeably different speech | A high interest in specific topics |
| Missing nonverbal communication cues like facial expressions | Noticeable distress when dealing with change or disruption |
| Exhibiting atypical social behavior, like not responding or walking away during a conversation | |

## Level 3: "Requiring Very Substantial Support"

Severe communication deficits, such as being nonspeaking

Repetitive behaviors like rocking or spinning

Extreme distress when asked to switch to a different task

They may need one-on-one time with an education assistant and may use augmentative and alternative communication (ACC) tools, like picture symbols.

Severe verbal and nonverbal social communication skills deficits are evident at this level. Individuals with Level 3 Autism have very limited initiation of social interactions and minimal response to social overtures from others. They might have very limited speech or, in some cases, be non-vocal. Understanding abstract concepts used in communication can be particularly challenging. Repetitive behaviors are more marked and can interfere significantly with functioning across all areas.

| Level 3: Social communication means the person may: | Level 3: Restricted interests and repetitive behavior traits can be: |
|---|---|
| Be nonspeaking or have echolalia (repeating words or phrases they hear) | Engage in repetitive physical behaviors like rocking, blinking, or spinning in circles |
| Prefer solitary activities | Express extreme distress when asked to switch tasks or focus |

Interact with others only to meet an immediate need

Seem unable to share imaginative play with peers

Demonstrate a limited interest in friendships

## Outside school activities any autistic child might benefit from are:

**01** Speech therapy

**02** Occupational therapy

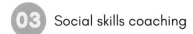

**03** Social skills coaching

**04** Applied behavior analysis (ABA) therapy

# OTHER TYPES OF AUTISM:

Autism Spectrum Disorder (ASD) is a complex neurodevelopmental condition that manifests in a variety of forms. It's important to note that the categorization of autism has evolved. The latest edition of the Diagnostic and Statistical Manual of Mental Disorders (DSM-5-TR) classifies autism as a single-spectrum disorder with varying levels of severity. However, historically and in common discourse, different types of autism have been recognized.

## 1. AUTISTIC DISORDER (CLASSIC AUTISM):

Traditionally known as "classic" autism, this form is what many people think of when they hear the word "autism." Significant social, communication, and behavioral challenges characterize it. Individuals with classic autism may have intellectual disabilities, limited language skills, and engage in repetitive behaviors. They might also have strong reactions to sensory inputs like light or sound.

## 2. ASPERGER'S SYNDROME (ASPERGER DISORDER):

Before it was integrated into the broader ASD diagnosis in the DSM-5, Asperger's Syndrome was considered a separate entity. Individuals with Asperger's typically exhibit milder symptoms of autism. They often have normal to above-average intelligence and don't have significant delays in language development. However, they usually experience difficulties in social interaction and may have narrowly focused interests and repetitive behaviors.

## 3. PERVASIVE DEVELOPMENTAL DISORDER - NOT OTHERWISE SPECIFIED (PDD-NOS):

This was a sort of catch-all category used for individuals who didn't fully meet the criteria for autistic disorder or Asperger's Syndrome. It was sometimes referred to as "atypical autism." Individuals with PDD-NOS might have exhibited some symptoms of autism, such as social and communication challenges, but not to the extent found in classic autism.

## 4. CHILDHOOD DISINTEGRATIVE DISORDER (CDD):

This rare form of autism is characterized by a severe regression in skills after several years of normal development. A child with CDD might develop normally until age 3 or 4, then rapidly lose language, motor, social, and other skills previously acquired.

## 5. RETT SYNDROME:

Initially considered part of the autism spectrum, Rett Syndrome is now recognized as a distinct genetic disorder. It primarily affects girls and is characterized by normal early growth and development followed by a slowing of development, loss of purposeful use of the hands, distinctive hand movements, slowed brain and head growth, problems with walking, seizures, and intellectual disability.

In the current understanding under the DSM-5-TR, these subtypes are no longer separately diagnosed. Instead, ASD is seen as a spectrum where each individual has a unique pattern of behavior and level of severity, from low to high functioning. The emphasis is on the individual's strengths and challenges, particularly in two core areas: social communication/interaction and restricted/repetitive behaviors.

Parents and caregivers must understand that regardless of where an individual falls on the spectrum, each person with ASD has their own set of strengths and challenges. The focus of intervention and support is on addressing their unique needs to help them lead fulfilling and productive lives. Understanding the different levels of ASD can help provide effective support and accommodations for individuals with this condition. It is important to remember that every person on the spectrum is unique and may not fit perfectly into these level descriptions.

*The information above was from the article "What Are The 3 Levels Of Autism?" By: Nancy Lovering*
*Link: https://psychcentral.com/autism/levels-of-autism#level-2*

# How ASD may impact Potty Training

Potty training can be a challenging process for any child, but for those with Autism Spectrum Disorder (ASD), it can be even more complicated. This section will explore the unique challenges children with ASD may face during toilet training. Understanding the fundamentals of ASD is essential to help parents and caregivers better support children on their potty training journey. From sensory challenges to communication difficulties, there are many factors to consider when it comes to toilet training for children with ASD. With patience, understanding, and the right strategies, parents and caregivers can help make the process of potty training a positive and successful experience for children with ASD.

As a behavior specialist with expertise in Applied Behavior Analysis (ABA) with children on the spectrum and a mother of a child with ASD, I know firsthand how difficult the process can be, especially for parents who aren't experienced in this field and first-time potty trainers. Luckily, I have created this book to help guide you through your potty training journey with your child. This is just another milestone that your child will have to face, and once your child gets past this milestone, you will feel accomplished. It took my son a whole year to learn the potty training process, and that was with consistency and a lot of patience.

You may be asking yourself, what if this doesn't work? What if I fail? What if my child isn't ready? All of these questions running through your head are normal, so don't be too hard on yourself. Potty training is a tough journey because it requires you to put your child in control, but it also shows them a form of independence. You provide them with the skills and resources, and then it is up to them to gain that control independently.

I wrote this book with first-time autism parents in mind who don't have the knowledge or resources to understand the behaviors of ASD children when it comes to potty training. I know how overwhelming and frustrating it can be to begin a journey like this. It takes a lot of patience and understanding. This book puts all the information you need to know in one place in order to be successful with your child. You will feel more prepared and confident to begin this potty training journey. Plus, you will find that this book will provide you with checklists, visual schedules, and resources to help guide you through your journey. My potty-training strategies will equip you with the tools, information, and mindset you need to be successful throughout the process. This book will guide you when facing challenges that most ASD children face throughout this process. It will also help you create the best potty training schedule suited for your child's needs. Just remember that every child is unique and faces different milestones/challenges. It is up to you to help guide them through the success based on their specific needs. You are their teacher. You make all the difference in how this potty training process will go. You are the one who will provide them with safety and boundaries, as well as create the structure they need to thrive. This book will be your guide every step of the way with a positive approach to help this process go as smoothly as possible. So, Let's get started!

# CHAPTER 2
# PREPARATION AND READINESS

# Recognizing Signs of Readiness

Recognizing when a child is ready for potty training is a key step for any parent, and several signs indicate your child might be prepared to start this important developmental journey. The readiness for potty training typically emerges between 18 months and three years, but it's important to remember that each child is unique and may show readiness at their own pace. One of the primary indicators is physical control and awareness; your child should be able to stay dry for at least two hours at a time during the day, which shows that their bladder muscles are sufficiently developed. Another physical sign is regular, predictable bowel movements. If your child consistently has bowel movements at similar times each day, it's a good sign they're ready for potty training. Additionally, being able to follow simple instructions, communicate their needs, and show an interest in bathroom habits, such as following others to the bathroom or expressing discomfort with dirty diapers, are key readiness indicators

Beyond physical readiness, emotional and psychological readiness are equally important. Children ready for potty training often desire independence and take pride in their accomplishments. They might express interest in wearing underwear instead of diapers or show curiosity about using the toilet. Your child must be at a stage where they can sit still for a few minutes at a time. It might not be the right time if they are resistant or fearful of the toilet. Potty training is a big step for children and can be challenging; they need to feel emotionally ready and not pressured. Parents must be patient and supportive, offering encouragement and praise for each small success. The process should be gradual and adapted to the child's pace. Pressuring a child to start potty training before they are ready can lead to setbacks and make the process more difficult for both the child and the parents.

# How do I know if my child is ready?

Determining your child's readiness for potty training involves looking for key indicators. Children typically show signs of readiness between 18 months and three years. These signs may include:

### 1. Interest in the toilet or potty chair:
Your child is curious about the toilet or potty chair and its use.

### 2. Understanding basic instructions:
Your child can follow simple instructions, indicating they may be ready to start potty training.

### 3.Uncomfortable in wet diapers:
Your child shows signs of discomfort when their diaper is wet or soiled.

### 4.Regular bowel movements:
Your child has predictable bowel movements.

### 5.Increased bladder control:
Your child stays dry longer during the day, indicating increased bladder control.

### 6.Ability to dress and undress:
Your child can pull down their pants and pull them up again, a skill necessary for potty training.

### 7.Communicates needs:
Your child begins to show or tell you when they need to go to the bathroom.

### 8.Desire for independence:
Your child shows a desire for independence and is eager to do things independently.

Remember, the key to successful potty training is patience and timing. Trying to rush a child who shows these signs of unreadiness can lead to frustration and setbacks. It's typically more effective to wait until the child shows more signs of readiness before beginning in earnest. Each child develops at their own pace, and what works for one child may not be appropriate for another.

Once you have determined that your child is showing signs of readiness, it's time to start the potty training. It's important to remember that this process may take some time and require patience and consistency from you and your child. Remember, every child is unique and may not show all these signs of readiness at once. Being patient and supportive as your child learns this new skill is important. It is a tough journey for parents with children on the spectrum, but it is a journey that will be worth it. It can take up to a few weeks, a few months, or maybe even a few years for an autistic child to learn how to use the potty properly, but if you stay consistent and positive, you can watch them thrive during this process. Every progress, even the little ones, is one that we should be celebrating. Like anything else, potty training takes practice and support from the parents. It is important to take a step back and let your child do their thing so that they can learn at their own pace. Be patient, consistent, and positive during this process. You got this!

# Tailoring approaches based on individuals' needs

Potty training is a significant milestone in a child's development, and for autistic individuals, a tailored approach is essential for success. With diverse needs and sensitivities, each person on the autism spectrum requires a unique strategy that aligns with their preferences and challenges.

Some of those approaches may include:

**01** Understanding Sensory Sensitivities

**02** Communication Styles and Alternatives

**03** Visual Supports and Social Stories

**04** Individualized Rewards System

**05** Gradual Exposure

**06** Structured Routine

**07** Respecting Individual Sensitivities

**08** Modeling and Social Learning

Potty training for autistic individuals is a journey that requires patience, understanding, and flexibility. Recognizing and respecting individual needs, incorporating personalized approaches, and collaborating with professionals, caregivers, and parents can create a positive and supportive environment for successful potty training. Remember, the key is to celebrate progress, no matter how small, and to adapt strategies for continued success.

# CHAPTER 3
# CREATING A STRUCTURED ENVIRONMENT

# Designing a sensory-friendly bathroom

Designing a sensory-friendly bathroom is crucial for children with Autism Spectrum Disorder (ASD) due to their unique sensory processing needs and challenges. Many autistic children are hypersensitive to sensory stimuli, which means that typical bathroom environments, with their echoing acoustics, bright lights, and varying textures, can be overwhelming or distressing. A sensory-friendly bathroom minimizes these stressors, creating a safe and comfortable space that can reduce anxiety and sensory overload. This adaptation is especially important considering the nature of bathroom activities, which require a level of comfort and relaxation for successful completion. For instance, a child who is less stressed by harsh lighting or loud flushing sounds is more likely to use the toilet and practice good hygiene successfully. Furthermore, incorporating elements like soft lighting, noise-reducing materials, and calming colors can make the bathroom a more inviting space, encouraging independence and self-care skills. This thoughtful environment not only supports the child's sensory needs but also fosters a sense of security and routine, which is particularly beneficial for children on the autism spectrum. By creating a sensory-friendly bathroom, we acknowledge and respect the individual experiences of autistic children, thereby promoting their overall well-being and daily functioning.

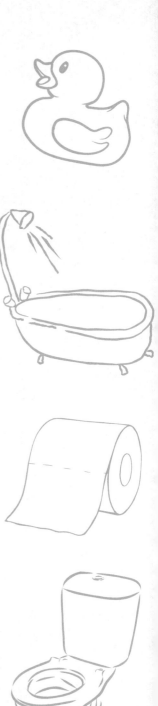

Designing a sensory-friendly bathroom for autistic children involves creating an environment that accommodates their sensory sensitivities and supports their comfort and independence. Here are some tips to help you design a sensory-friendly bathroom:

### 1. Soft Lighting:
Opt for soft, natural lighting to create a calming atmosphere. Consider installing dimmer switches to adjust the brightness based on the child's preferences.

### 2. Neutral Colors:
Use neutral and calming colors on the walls and accessories. Avoid overly bright or contrasting colors that may be overwhelming. Earth tones and pastels are often well-received.

### 3. Sensory-Friendly Textures:
Introduce sensory-friendly textures, such as soft tissue paper and rugs. Consider adding textured wall decals or wallpaper to create visual interest without being too stimulating.

### 4. Comfortable Seating:
Use a child-sized toilet seat with a reducer that's easily removable. This provides more comfort while your child uses the toilet.

### 5. Noise Reduction Measures:
Implement noise reduction measures, such as adding soft materials like curtains or rugs to absorb sound. Noise-canceling features on ventilation systems or using calming background music can also be beneficial.

### 6. Visual Supports:

Incorporate visual supports, such as visual schedules or cues, to guide the child through bathroom routines. This helps establish a clear sequence of activities.

### 7. Safety Features:

Lockable cabinets for medications or cleaning supplies, anti-scald devices on taps, and corner protectors for sharp edges. Provide a non-slip stool or steps for reaching the sink or toilet safely.

### 8. Privacy and Routine:

Ensure that the bathroom provides privacy and establishes a consistent routine for bathroom breaks. Predictability helps reduce anxiety and promotes a sense of control.

### 9. Aromatherapy Options:

Explore subtle aromatherapy options, such as mild scents or essential oil diffusers. Ensure that the chosen scents are not overpowering and are well-tolerated by the child.

### 10. Feedback and Adaptation:

Regularly seek feedback from the child and be open to adapting the sensory-friendly features based on their evolving needs and preferences.

Here are some additional ideas for a more sensory friendly bathroom:

### 11. Non-Slip Flooring:

Choose non-slip flooring to enhance safety. This provides a stable surface and reduces the risk of slips or falls, promoting security.

### 12. Adjustable Showerheads:

You can install an adjustable showerhead to customize water pressure and temperature. This provides flexibility to accommodate sensory preferences related to water flow.

### 13.Organization and Predictability:

Keep the bathroom well-organized to provide a sense of predictability. Use labeled bins or baskets for toiletries and other items, making locating what they need easy for the child.

### 14. Customized Toiletries:

Allow the child to choose preferred toiletries, such as soaps and shampoos. Consider sensory-friendly options, such as fragrance-free products.

### 15. Personalized Decor:

Decorate the bathroom with personalized items that the child enjoys. This could include themed accessories or artwork that align with their interests.

Remember that each child is unique, so tailor the sensory-friendly bathroom to the individual's specific sensory profile and preferences. Regular communication and observation will help fine-tune the environment for the child's comfort and well-being.

# Establishing routines and creating a schedule

Establishing routines during potty time is particularly beneficial for autistic children, as consistency and predictability can significantly ease the stress associated with learning new skills. Children on the autism spectrum often thrive with structured routines, providing a sense of security and order. When it comes to potty training, creating a regular schedule - such as taking the child to the bathroom consistently throughout the day - helps develop a natural rhythm and expectation for bathroom use. Utilizing visual aids, like

picture schedules or charts, can further assist in this process by providing clear, visual cues about when it's time to use the toilet. Consistency in the steps involved in using the bathroom - such as flushing, washing hands, and using the same amount of toilet paper - can also be comforting and make the process more manageable for the child. It's important to integrate these routines calmly and non-rushedly and pair them with positive reinforcement to encourage cooperation and success. Personalizing the routine to fit your child's specific needs and preferences while remaining flexible to adjustments is key. This structured approach not only aids in successfully acquiring toileting skills but also promotes a sense of accomplishment and independence in autistic children, fostering their overall development and self-confidence.

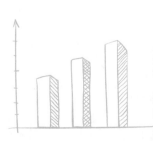

"**Trip Training**" and "**Schedule Training**" are terms used in the context of potty training for autistic children. Both approaches involve creating structured routines can help your child to develop consistent bathroom habits. Let's explore each concept:

## 1. Trip. Training

Trip training involves taking your child to the bathroom regularly throughout the day, regardless of whether they indicate the need to go. This proactive approach is designed to establish a routine and reduce the likelihood of accidents. The intervals are typically predetermined and may be based on factors such as the child's age, the time since their last bathroom visit, or known patterns of when they are likely to need to use the toilet.

### KEY FEATURES OF TRIP TRAINING:

- **Consistency:** The child is taken to the bathroom consistently at set intervals.
- **Proactive Approach:** It does not rely on the child signaling when they need to go but instead anticipates their bathroom needs.
- **Establishing Routine:** The goal is to establish a predictable bathroom routine to foster awareness and control.

> You want to use the Trip Training Method if your child is just getting used to the toilet.

Example: Set a goal for eight toilet sits per day. At first, trips will be short (as little as 10 seconds per trip). Over time, toilet sits can be long (e.g., up to 5 minutes). Setting a timer can be a helpful way to let your child know when the toilet sit can end. Your child can also get up from the toilet immediately if s/he urinates or has a bowel movement. Boys are taught to sit on the toilet to urinate until they regularly have bowel movements on the toilet.

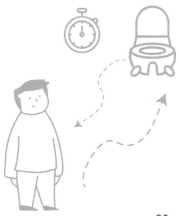

## 2. Schedule Training:

Schedule training is similar to trip training but involves setting a specific schedule for bathroom visits based on the child's daily routine. This approach considers the child's natural patterns, such as eating, drinking, or engaging in specific activities. The schedule is customized to the child's individual habits and aims to align with their body's natural rhythms.

### KEY FEATURES OF TRIP TRAINING:

- **Individualized Schedule:** The bathroom schedule is tailored to the child's unique routine and habits.
- **Routine Integration:** Bathroom breaks are integrated into the child's daily schedule, promoting a sense of predictability.
- **Observation and Adjustment:** The schedule may be adjusted based on observations of the child's response and the success of the training.

> You want to use the Schedule Training once your child develops a routine.

### INDIVIDUALIZATION AND FLEXIBILITY:

It's crucial to emphasize that each child is unique, and what works for one may not work for another. The success of trip training or schedule training depends on the child's individual needs, preferences, and developmental stage. Additionally, flexibility is key, and caregivers may need to adapt the approach based on the child's progress and feedback.

Both trip training and schedule training are strategies that recognize the importance of routine and structure in facilitating successful potty training for autistic children. The chosen approach should align with the child's characteristics and be implemented with patience, consistency, and positive reinforcement.

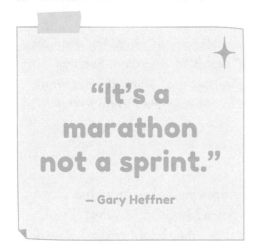

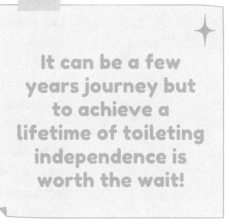

A study by Dalrymple and Ruble (1992) found that, on average, children with ASD require 1.6 years of toilet training to stay dry during the day and sometimes more than 2 years to achieve bowel control.

## CREATING YOUR CHILD'S TOILETING PLAN:

Creating a toileting plan for your autistic child involves thoughtful consideration of their individual needs, preferences, and developmental stage. A written toileting plan may help your autistic child make progress. If it is in writing, everyone will be able to use the same language and the same routine. Toileting plans may include these details:

| Goals | Routine |
|---|---|
| What are you trying to achieve for the given period? For example, "The goal is to have Luiz visit the restroom 30 minutes throughout the day and sit on the toilet for at least 10 seconds." | How often? Include how often or what time the child should visit the restroom. Some examples include "every hour on the hour" or "15 minutes after drinking / meals." |

For how long? Be sure to include how long your child can tolerate the bathroom trips-it may start with only 10 seconds.

## LANGUAGE:

Use words that work for your child. For example, use any "code" words for urination. Such as "Potty, Toilet, PeePee, etc." Think of what words you would use to tell your child to go to the bathroom.

## PLACES:

**Where?** Where does your child go to the bathroom? At home? At School? **What?** Think about the lights; are they bright or dim? How does light affect your child? What about noises in the bathroom (e.g., a fan)? What about the type of toilet paper? Should the door be open or closed? **Who?** Who goes with your child to the bathroom? Teacher? Therapist? Grandparent?

## TOOLS:

What tools are you using? Do you use a visual schedule? Does your child like to listen to music or read a book?

## REWARDS:

This is a big one! What activities earn a reward? What activities do not? How do you reward your child for a job well done? What happens if your child does not earn a reward? Is the reward delayed or immediate?

You would need to consider these things when creating your potty training routine.

# 6 Methods to Help You Build Your Routine:

1.  Tell your child when to go to the bathroom; don't ask them. Just take them every 30 minutes. Timers help not only your child but it will help remind you that it's time to take them to the potty.

2.  Make toilet trips part of your everyday life. Plan toilet trips around your usual routine. Stick with the same times of the day or the same daily activities.

3.  Use the same simple words, signs, or pictures during each trip. This helps your child learn the toileting language.

4.  They say it takes three weeks to make a habit. Once you outline the routine and methods, keep working towards the same goal for three weeks.

5.  Make a visual schedule! Take pictures of your bathroom to make it more individualized and personal.

6.  Identify Rewards that your child would like to earn for using the potty. Think of which ones will be easiest to give your child as soon as he/she urinates or has a bowel movement in the toilet. A small food item (e.g., fruit snack, cracker, skittle) often works well. In addition to giving a reward for "going" in the toilet, you can also give your child time to do a favorite activity (e.g., watch a video or play with a toy) after the toilet trip. You also want to make sure you are providing verbal praise every time. For example: "Good job going pee pee in the toilet!"

# Establishing a nighttime routine

Nighttime potty training can be a challenging milestone for any child, and when your child is on the autism spectrum, it may require additional strategies and support. Establishing a successful nighttime routine is essential for promoting independence, ensuring restful sleep, and maintaining good hygiene. Here are effective nighttime potty training routines for autistic individuals, what to look out for, and how to build a routine that works for your child and family.

## Understanding the Importance of a Routine:

A consistent nighttime routine provides structure and predictability, which can be especially comforting for children with autism who thrive on routine. Start by establishing a regular bedtime and wake-up time to regulate your child's sleep-wake cycle. Consistency is key; aim to maintain the same bedtime and wake-up time every day, even on weekends. A structured routine can help signal to your child's body that it's time to wind down and prepare for sleep.

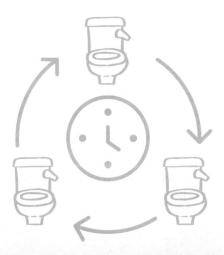

# Building a Nighttime Potty Training Routine:

A consistent nighttime routine provides structure and predictability, which can be especially comforting for children with autism who thrive on routine. Start by establishing a regular bedtime and wake-up time to regulate your child's sleep-wake cycle. Consistency is key; aim to maintain the same bedtime and wake-up time every day, even on weekends. A structured routine can help signal to your child's body that it's time to wind down and prepare for sleep.

### Limit Fluid Intake Before Bed:
Encourage your child to drink fluids earlier in the evening and avoid caffeinated beverages close to bedtime.

### Establish a Pre-Bedtime Routine:
Create a calming pre-bedtime routine that includes activities like brushing teeth, changing into pajamas, and reading a book. This routine signals to your child that it's almost time for bed.

### Use the Bathroom Before Bed:
Encourage your child to use the bathroom before getting into bed to empty their bladder. Make sure the bathroom is well-lit and inviting, and consider using a nightlight if your child is afraid of the dark.

### Provide Supportive Bedding:
Invest in waterproof mattress covers and protective bedding to manage accidents and make cleanup easier. Consider using absorbent undergarments or training pants designed for nighttime use.

### Encourage Self-Regulation:

Teach your child to recognize their body's signals for needing to use the bathroom during the night. Encourage them to wake up and use the bathroom independently if they feel the urge.

### Reward Success:

Celebrate your child's successes and progress with positive reinforcement. Consider using a sticker chart or reward system to motivate and encourage nighttime dryness.

### Be Patient and Persistent:

Nighttime potty training may take time and patience, so be prepared for setbacks and accidents along the way. Stay consistent with your routine and offer plenty of encouragement and support to your child.

# What to Look Out For:

- **Bedwetting:** Bedwetting is common in children, especially those who are still developing nighttime bladder control. If your child continues to wet the bed frequently despite your efforts, consult with a healthcare professional to rule out any underlying medical issues.

- **Disturbed Sleep**: Pay attention to signs of disturbed sleep, such as restlessness, frequent waking, or difficulty falling asleep. These may indicate discomfort or anxiety related to nighttime potty training.

- **Emotional Response**: Notice your child's emotional response to nighttime potty training. If they seem anxious, frustrated, or stressed, consider adjusting your approach to make the process more comfortable and supportive for them.

Nighttime potty training for individuals with autism requires patience, consistency, and understanding. By establishing a structured nighttime routine, providing support and encouragement, and being attentive to your child's needs, you can help them develop nighttime bladder control and promote restful sleep. Remember to celebrate their successes and progress along the way, and seek guidance from healthcare professionals if needed. With time and perseverance, nighttime potty training can become a successful and empowering milestone for your child.

# CHAPTER 4
# COMMUNICATION STRATEGIES

# Developing effective communication with non-verbal children

Effective communication with non-verbal children during potty time is vital to successful toilet training. Since these children may not use traditional verbal language, alternative methods of communication are essential. Visual aids, such as picture cards or symbols representing the bathroom, can be incredibly useful. These can help the child understand and signal their need to use the toilet. Consistent use of these aids can create a clear and understandable routine. Moreover, paying close attention to the child's body language and cues is crucial, as these may indicate their need to go to the bathroom. Non-verbal cues can range from certain facial expressions to specific body movements or gestures. It's also beneficial to establish a regular bathroom schedule to reduce the need for the child to communicate urgency, which can be challenging for them. Incorporating a reward system that positively reinforces their successful communication efforts can encourage repetition of the desired behavior. Throughout this process, patience and consistent, positive reinforcement are key. By creating an environment of understanding and responsiveness to their unique ways of communicating, caregivers can significantly ease the potty-training process for non-verbal children, aiding in their comfort and development.

Communication barriers can add complexity to the process, making it crucial for parents and caregivers to implement strategies that cater to the unique needs of their children.

### UNDERSTANDING INDIVIDUAL NEEDS:

Non-verbal autistic children often experience the world in distinctive ways. Before embarking on the toilet training journey, it's crucial to understand the child's sensory preferences, sensitivities, and communication style. Observing their reactions to different textures, sounds, and routines provides valuable insights into crafting a personalized approach.

### VISUAL SUPPORTS AND SCHEDULES:

Visual aids play a pivotal role in helping non-verbal autistic children understand routines. Create visual schedules or use picture cards to illustrate the toilet's steps. This provides a clear and tangible guide for your child, helping them anticipate and understand the process. Social stories, accompanied by simple and clear visuals, can help prepare the child for what to expect and establish a sense of routine.

### ESTABLISHING A CONSISTENT ROUTINE:

Routine is essential for non-verbal autistic children. Establishing a consistent toilet training routine helps create a sense of predictability. Set specific times for bathroom breaks, such as after meals or upon waking. Consistency across different environments, such as home and school, reinforces the routine and facilitates generalization of skills.

### SENSORY CONSIDERATIONS:

Take into account sensory sensitivities during toilet training. Ensure that the bathroom environment is comfortable and accommodating. If certain textures or sounds are distressing, explore alternatives such as using flushable wipes or adjusting the lighting in the bathroom.

### OFFER CHOICES:

Provide your child with choices throughout the toilet training process. Allow them to choose aspects like the color of the potty or the type of toilet paper. Offering choices empowers your child and gives them a sense of control.

### POSITIVE REINFORCEMENT AND REWARDS:

Non-verbal autistic children may find it challenging to understand verbal praise alone. Utilize tangible and immediate reinforcements such as stickers, small treats, or a favorite toy to reward successful attempts at using the toilet. Be consistent in linking positive reinforcement to desired behaviors.

### MODELING BEHAVIOR:

Children learn through observation. Demonstrate the steps of using the toilet by modeling the behavior yourself. This visual cue can be especially helpful for non-verbal children who may learn by watching others.

### COMMUNICATION STRATEGIES:

Explore alternative communication methods for expressing bathroom needs. This may include using signs, symbols, or picture cards. Encourage the child to communicate their needs in a way that is comfortable and natural for them. Consistent positive reinforcement for communication efforts helps build confidence.

### BEHAVIORAL STRATEGIES:

Addressing challenging behaviors is an integral part of toilet training. Patience and understanding are essential. Implement positive behavior modification techniques and seek guidance from professionals experienced in working with non-verbal autistic children. Focus on reinforcing positive behaviors rather than punitive measures.

### COLLABORATION WITH PROFESSIONALS:

Collaborate with a team of professionals, including speech therapists, occupational therapists, and behavioral specialists. Their expertise can provide valuable insights and support tailored to the child's unique needs. Regular communication with professionals ensures a holistic approach to toilet training.

### CELEBRATING PROGRESS AND PATIENCE:

Toilet training is a journey marked by progress and setbacks. Celebrate small victories, no matter how insignificant they may seem. Patience is key, and acknowledging the child's efforts, no matter how small, contributes to a positive and encouraging atmosphere.

Toilet training non-verbal autistic children requires a combination of understanding, patience, and personalized strategies. Caregivers can navigate this journey with empathy and success by taking into account individual needs, utilizing visual supports, and fostering effective communication. Every step forward is a triumph, bringing the child and their caregivers closer to this significant milestone.

# Importance of Visual Supports:

Effective communication with non-verbal children during potty time is vital to successful toilet training. Since these children may not use traditional verbal language, alternative methods of communication are essential. Visual aids, such as picture cards or symbols representing the bathroom, can be incredibly useful. These can help the child understand and signal their need to use the toilet. Consistent use of these aids can create a clear and understandable routine. Moreover, paying close attention to the child's body language and cues is crucial, as these may indicate their need to go to the bathroom. Non-verbal cues can range from certain facial expressions to specific body movements or gestures. It's also beneficial to establish a regular bathroom schedule to reduce the need for the child to communicate urgency, which can be challenging for them. Incorporating a reward system that positively reinforces their successful communication efforts can encourage repetition of the desired behavior. Throughout this process, patience and consistent, positive reinforcement are key. By creating an environment of understanding and responsiveness to their unique ways of communicating, caregivers can significantly ease the potty-training process for non-verbal children, aiding in their comfort and development.

# Importance of Social Stories:

Social stories play a crucial role in facilitating a positive and understandable experience during potty time for autistic children. These personalized narratives help break down the complex process of using the toilet into clear, sequential steps, providing a visual and written guide tailored to the child's specific needs. Social stories can include details about recognizing the sensation of needing to use the bathroom, the steps involved in using the toilet, and the importance of hygiene routines like washing hands. By presenting information in a story format, with relatable characters and situations, social stories make the abstract concept of potty training more concrete and accessible to autistic children. This storytelling approach helps address their potential challenges in understanding abstract or unfamiliar situations, making the potty training process less daunting and more predictable. Social stories can also be used to introduce the idea of using the toilet in various settings, promoting generalization of the skill. The visual and narrative components of social stories offer valuable support in preparing autistic children for the expectations and routines associated with potty time, fostering a sense of comfort, predictability, and, ultimately, successful toileting experiences.

# Words to use during Potty Training

Using positive phrases and words during the potty training process with autistic children is essential for creating a supportive and comfortable environment that promotes learning and reduces anxiety. Autistic children often thrive on routine, clear communication, and positive reinforcement. Positive language helps to reinforce desired behaviors, build confidence, and maintain their motivation throughout the process. By focusing on their efforts and progress, rather than mistakes or challenges, positive phrases encourage them to continue trying and help to establish a positive association with potty training. Additionally, positive reinforcement can help mitigate any sensory sensitivities or anxieties that autistic children may experience during potty training, fostering a sense of safety and trust in the learning environment. Overall, using positive phrases and words is instrumental in facilitating a successful and empowering potty training journey for autistic children.

When guiding an autistic child through the potty training journey, clear, positive, and supportive communication is key. Here are some phrases that can help create a more comfortable and encouraging environment for them:

### 1. "YOU DID A GREAT JOB SITTING ON THE POTTY!

Celebrating even the small steps can boost their confidence and willingness to continue trying.

### 2. "WOULD YOU LIKE TO CHOOSE A BOOK OR TOY TO TAKE WITH US?"

Offering choices gives them a sense of control and makes the experience more enjoyable.

### 3. "LOOK HOW DRY YOU ARE! THAT'S FANTASTIC!"

Recognizing and praising their progress, such as staying dry, encourages them to keep up their efforts.

### 4. "THIS IS YOUR SPECIAL POTTY CHART. LET'S ADD A STICKER FOR TRYING TODAY!"

Using visual tools like progress charts with stickers or marks can make achievements tangible and motivating.

### 5. "WOULD YOU LIKE TO FLUSH THE TOILET? IT'S OKAY IF NOT."

Giving them the option to engage in different aspects of the process empowers them to participate to the extent they're comfortable.

### 6. "FIRST WE USE THE POTTY, THEN WE CAN [PREFERRED ACTIVITY]."

Using simple "first...then..." statements can help establish a routine and make the process more predictable, which is often comforting for autistic children.

### 7. "IT'S OKAY TO FEEL [EMOTION]. WE CAN TRY AGAIN WHEN YOU'RE READY."

Validating their feelings, whether it's frustration, fear, or reluctance, shows empathy and understanding, making them feel supported.

### 8. "I SEE YOU'RE UPSET. LET'S TAKE A DEEP BREATH TOGETHER."

Offering strategies to manage emotions can be helpful, especially if the child becomes overwhelmed or distressed.

### 9. "WOULD YOU LIKE THE LIGHT ON OR OFF? DO YOU WANT THE DOOR OPEN OR CLOSED?"

Allowing them to make choices about their environment can reduce anxiety and give them a sense of control during the process.

### 10. "WE CAN USE THE TIMER TO REMIND US WHEN IT'S TIME TO TRY THE POTTY AGAIN."

Using a timer can help make transitions smoother and the concept of time more tangible.

### 11. "LET'S PUT YOUR POTTY SCHEDULE ON THE WALL WHERE YOU CAN SEE IT.

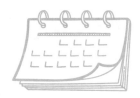

Visual schedules can help autistic children understand and anticipate what comes next, reducing anxiety around the unknown.

### 12. "YOU'RE WORKING HARD ON LEARNING HOW TO USE THE POTTY. I'M PROUD OF YOU."

Affirming their effort rather than just the outcome acknowledges the work they're putting into the process.

### 13. "THIS IS YOUR SPECIAL POTTY SONG. LET'S SING IT TOGETHER!"

Incorporating a song or rhyme can make potty time more

### 14. "LET'S TAKE A BREAK AND TRY AGAIN IN A LITTLE WHILE."

Acknowledging the need for breaks can prevent them from feeling overwhelmed and help maintain a positive association with potty training.

### 15. "YOU CAN TELL ME OR SHOW ME WHEN YOU NEED TO GO. HERE'S A PICTURE WE CAN USE."

Providing visual aids or simple cues can help them communicate their needs, especially if they are non-verbal or have limited verbal communication.

By tailoring your approach and language to your autistic child's needs, you can provide them with the structure, encouragement, and support necessary to navigate potty training successfully.

# Words NOT to use during Potty Training

### 1. "DON'T WORRY- I'LL CLEAN IT UP!"

We should strive to involve our children in cleaning up their accident to promote independence.

Instead try saying, "I will grab some paper towels and you can help me clean it up."

### 2. "DO YOU WANT TO GO POTTY? OR DO YOU HAVE TO GO POTTY?"

Most of our children won't understand this question or they will say "No" 9 times out of 10 because they maybe doing something more enjoyable than using the potty like eating a snack or playing with a toy.

Instead try saying, It's time to go potty!" or "First we go potty then we can play with toys."

### 3. "I'M SO FRUSTRATED."

Try not to show that you are frustrated because our children can sense that. Instead try taking a deep breath and just remember to be patient.

breathe

## 4. "HURRY UP"

This can cause stress and pressure, making it difficult for the child to relax and use the potty successfully.   38

Instead try saying, "I will set a timer for one minute."

## 5. "YOU SHOULD KNOW HOW TO DO THIS"

This assumes a level of intuitive understanding that the child may not have, making them feel inadequate.

Instead try saying, "It's okay we will keep practicing."

## 6. "JUST" PHRASES (E.G., "JUST GO TO THE BATHROOM")

Using "just" can oversimplify the process for the child, disregarding the challenges they may face.

Instead try saying, "Let's go use the bathroom!"

## 7. "WHY CAN'T YOU BE LIKE [OTHER CHILD]?"

Comparisons can diminish self-esteem and ignore the unique challenges and pace of each child's development.

Instead try saying, "I can see you are doing the best that you can and I am so proud of you!"

## 8. "DON'T BE SCARED"

This dismisses their feelings. Acknowledge their fear and provide reassurance instead.

Instead try saying, "It is okay to feel scared."

## 9. "YOU ALWAYS/NEVER..."

Absolute terms can reinforce negative perceptions of their abilities and discourage them from trying.

Instead try saying, "Let's try sitting on the toilet with a calm body."

## 10. "YOU DID IT WRONG."

Instead of focusing on what the child did wrong, it's more helpful to gently guide them on how to do it right next time, offering support and encouragement.

Instead try saying, "You got this!"

## 11. "YOU'VE RUINED YOUR CLOTHES AGAIN!"

This phrase emphasizes the negative outcome (soiled clothes) rather than focusing on the learning process. It can create feelings of shame and discourage the child from trying again.

Instead try saying, "Accidents happen and that is okay."

## 12. "I'LL GIVE YOU A TREAT IF YOU USE THE POTTY."

While rewards can be motivating, relying too heavily on them can teach children to perform behaviors only when a reward is offered, rather than learning the intrinsic value of the behavior.

Instead try saying, "Once you earn your token you can choose your reward."

## 13. "YOU'RE TOO OLD FOR DIAPERS."

This can create shame around wearing diapers, making the child feel embarrassed about their current stage of development, rather than focusing on the positive goal of learning to use the potty.

Instead try saying, "Lets try putting underwear over your pull ups."

## 14. "IF YOU USE THE POTTY, YOU'RE A GOOD KID."

This conditions their worth on their ability to use the potty, which can be particularly damaging for autistic children who may take longer to learn this skill. Their value should not be tied to their potty training success.

Instead try saying, "Good job trying to use the potty!"

## 15. "JUST HOLD IT UNTIL YOU GET TO THE TOILET."

For some autistic children, understanding and responding to bodily sensations in time can be difficult. This phrase may not only be unrealistic but also increase pressure and anxiety.

Instead try saying, *"It is okay to have accidents."*

When communicating with an autistic child about potty training, it's important to be patient, clear, and supportive. Recognize their efforts, provide consistent encouragement, and understand that their path to learning this skill might differ from others.

# CHAPTER 5
# POSITIVE REINFORCEMENT TECHNIQUES

# Identifying suitable rewards:

Choosing suitable rewards for potty training is essential, as positive reinforcement can motivate and encourage children to develop good bathroom habits. When identifying rewards, it's important to consider the child's preferences, individual sensitivities, and age-appropriateness. Here are some tips on how to identify suitable rewards for potty training:

### 1. Individual Preferences:

Take into account the child's interests and preferences. What motivates one child may not work for another. Consider favorite activities, characters, toys, or hobbies when selecting rewards.

### 2. Immediate and Tangible:

Choose rewards that are immediate and tangible. Children, especially younger ones, may have difficulty understanding delayed gratification. Small and immediate rewards provide a clear connection between the behavior and the positive outcome. Ex: favorite snack, or access to iPad.

### 3. Variety of Rewards:

Offer a variety of rewards to keep the motivation high. This prevents the child from becoming bored or disinterested in a particular incentive. Rotate between different types of rewards to maintain excitement.

### 4. Age-Appropriate:

Ensure that the rewards are age-appropriate. Younger children may be motivated by simple stickers, while older children may prefer more complex incentives such as a special outing or additional playtime.

### 5. Praise and Recognition:

Verbal praise is a powerful form of reinforcement. Celebrate the child's achievements with positive words and enthusiastic encouragement. Combine verbal praise with tangible rewards to reinforce the positive behavior.

### 6. Involvement in Reward Selection:

Involve the child in selecting their rewards. This empowers them and makes the process more enjoyable. Offer choices and let them express their preferences, fostering a sense of ownership in the process.

### 7. Consistency in Rewarding:

Be consistent in rewarding desired behaviors. This helps reinforce the connection between using the potty and receiving a reward. Consistency is key to establishing positive habits.

### 8. Special Privileges:

Consider offering special privileges as rewards. This could include additional playtime, choosing a favorite activity, or having a special treat. These privileges can serve as powerful motivators.

### 9. Celebratory Events:

Plan special celebratory events for significant milestones. For example, reaching a week of successful potty training could be rewarded with a small party, a special outing, or a favorite meal.

### 10. Avoid Overly Sugary Treats:

While occasional treats can be motivating, it's important to avoid excessive use of sugary rewards. Balancing rewards with healthier options or non-food incentives is advisable for the child's overall well-being.

### 11. Monitor Effectiveness:

Pay attention to the child's response to different rewards. If a particular incentive loses its effectiveness, be open to adjusting the rewards to maintain motivation.

Remember that each child is unique, and what works for one may not work for another. It's crucial to observe the child's reactions and adapt the reward system based on their individual preferences and needs. Positive reinforcement, coupled with patience and consistency, can contribute to a successful and positive potty training experience.

# Implementing reinforcement schedules

Implementing reinforcement schedules during potty time for autistic children is crucial for creating a positive and motivating environment. These children often respond well to structured routines and benefit from clear cause-and-effect relationships. A reinforcement schedule involves consistently rewarding desired behaviors, such as using the toilet independently or following the steps of the toileting routine. The rewards can be tailored to the child's preferences and may include praise, small treats, or special privileges. Using a reinforcement schedule encourages the repetition of successful behaviors and helps establish a connection between positive actions and positive outcomes. This positive reinforcement creates a sense of achievement and boosts the child's confidence during the challenging potty training process. Additionally, a well-implemented reinforcement schedule can serve as a powerful tool in reducing anxiety and resistance associated with toileting, making the experience more enjoyable and reinforcing the development of essential self-care skills. By consistently pairing potty training efforts with positive reinforcement, caregivers can create a supportive and encouraging atmosphere, fostering a more successful and comfortable potty training journey for autistic children.

Implementing a reinforcement schedule can be tough at first. The most important thing to remember is to reinforce your child right away. For example, If your child's goal is to sit on the toilet for 20 seconds and they achieve that goal, provide the reinforcing item immediately.

Make sure to have multiple reinforcing items for your child to choose from. Don't just stick with one because they can get satiated with that item, which will no longer motivate them. So, continuously alternate the reinforcement.

Consistency is crucial for the success of a reinforcement schedule. Ensure that all caregivers and individuals involved are on the same page and consistently follow the established schedule.

**TIPS FOR PARENTS:**

- Be patient and positive throughout the process.
- Provide clear and simple instructions for the behavior you're reinforcing.
- Celebrate even small successes to keep your child motivated.
- Use visuals or social stories to help explain the process to your child.

Remember that each child is unique, so it's essential to tailor the reinforcement schedule to your child's needs and preferences. Positive reinforcement and a supportive and consistent approach contribute to a successful potty training experience.

# How To Implement A Token Board

Potty training an autistic child presents unique challenges and requires approaches that cater to their specific needs for structure, predictability, and motivation. One effective method that stands out for its adaptability and positive reinforcement principles is the use of a token board. This visual and interactive tool can significantly ease the potty training process by breaking down the task into manageable steps, offering clear visual cues, and rewarding desired behaviors in a way that resonates with autistic children. By utilizing a token board, parents can create a supportive and encouraging environment that not only aids in achieving potty training milestones but also enhances the child's understanding of cause and effect, delays gratification, and fosters a sense of accomplishment. This introduction will guide parents on how to implement a token board effectively during their autistic child's potty training journey, providing a structured approach that aligns with their child's learning style and preferences.

## 1. DESIGN THE TOKEN BOARD:

- **Select a Theme:** Choose a board theme that interests the child, such as favorite animals, characters, or colors.
- **Determine the Size:** The board should have enough space for the number of tokens that will be earned towards a specific reward.
- **Create Tokens:** Tokens can be anything from stickers, stars, to custom-made tokens related to the theme. Ensure they are visually appealing to the child.

## 2. DEFINE THE DESIRED BEHAVIORS

- **Identify Specific Behaviors:** Clearly define the behaviors or tasks you want to encourage. For potty training, this might include sitting on the toilet, using the toilet, washing hands, etc.
- **Set Clear Goals:** Make sure these behaviors are achievable and understandable for the child. Break down tasks into smaller steps if necessary.

## 3. CHOOSE THE REWARDS

- **Select Meaningful Rewards:** Choose rewards that are highly motivating for the child. These can range from activities (like extra playtime) to tangible items (small toys or favorite snacks).
- **Vary the Rewards:** Having a variety of rewards can help maintain the child's interest in earning tokens.

## 4. EXPLAIN THE SYSTEM TO THE CHILD

- **Use Simple Language:** Explain how the token board works in a clear, concise way that the child can understand. Visual aids or demonstrations can be helpful.
- **Role-play:** Demonstrate the process of earning a token and exchanging tokens for rewards to ensure the child understands the concept.

## 5. IMPLEMENT THE TOKEN BOARD

- **Consistency:** Use the token board consistently every time the child engages in the target behavior. This reinforces the connection between the behavior and the reward.
- **Immediate Reinforcement:** Give the token immediately after the desired behavior to reinforce the action. Delayed rewards might not be as effective.

## 6. CELEBRATE SUCCESS

- **Positive Reinforcement:** Offer praise and excitement every time a token is earned and especially when a reward is achieved. This enhances the positive experience.
- **Share Achievements:** Encourage the child to share their success with other family members or caregivers to further reinforce their achievement.

## 7. REVIEW AND ADJUST

- **Monitor Progress:** Keep track of how well the token board is working. Is the child motivated? Are the behaviors improving?
- **Make Adjustments:** If necessary, adjust the behaviors, token amount needed for rewards, or the rewards themselves to maintain or increase effectiveness.

## 8. PROVIDE SUPPORT

- **Encourage the Child:** Support and encouragement are key. Focus on effort as much as achievement.
- **Parental Patience:** Remind parents to be patient and persistent. Progress might be slow, but consistency and positive reinforcement can lead to success.

## 9. EXPAND OR PHASE OUT

- **Expand:** As the child masters specific behaviors, new behaviors can be added to the token board to continue their development.
- **Phase Out:** Gradually, as behaviors become consistent, start phasing out the token system for those behaviors while potentially introducing new goals.

Token boards can be a powerful tool in supporting the development of positive behaviors in autistic children. By following these steps, parents can effectively implement this strategy to aid in potty training and beyond, adapting it as needed to fit their child's unique needs and progress.

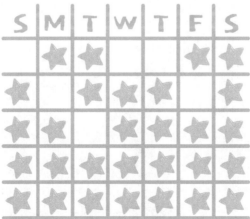

# CHAPTER 6
# HANDLING CHALLENGES AND SENSORY ISSUES

*DID YOU KNOW THAT AROUND 80% OF CHILDREN EXPERIENCE SETBACKS DURING THE POTTY TRAINING PROCESS?"*

# Addressing sensory sensitivities during potty time:

Incorporating sensory activities during potty time for autistic children is paramount for creating a comfortable and supportive environment that addresses their unique sensory needs. Many autistic children experience sensory sensitivities or seek specific sensory input, and the bathroom can be challenging due to its inherent sensory stimuli. By adding sensory activities, such as using scented soaps, providing soft towels, or incorporating calming lighting, caregivers can help make the bathroom more tolerable and enjoyable. These sensory enhancements can distract from potential stressors, making the overall toileting experience more positive. Additionally, sensory activities can act as cues, signaling the child that it's time for a specific task, like washing hands after using the toilet. The incorporation of sensory elements not only makes potty time more manageable for autistic children but also contributes to their overall sensory integration, potentially reducing anxiety and fostering a more relaxed and successful potty training process.

Addressing sensory sensitivities during potty time is crucial, especially for children with autism who may have heightened sensitivities to certain objects. Here are some strategies to help make the potty time experience more comfortable for children with sensory sensitivities:

### Individual Preferences:

 Ensure the bathroom is well-lit and the temperature is comfortable. Some children may be sensitive to bright lights or cold environments. Consider using soft lighting or adding a space heater if necessary. Please refer to the previous module on *"Creating a sensory-friendly environment"*

### Offer a Choice of Toilet Paper:

Some children have sensory preferences for the texture of toilet paper. Offer a choice between different types of toilet paper (e.g., soft, flushable wipes) to accommodate their sensory needs.

### Provide Familiar Toiletries:

Use familiar and preferred toiletries, such as soap, hand sanitizer, or lotion. This can help create a sensory-friendly experience and make the child feel more at ease.

### Use a Potty Chair:

Consider using a potty chair instead of the regular toilet. Potty chairs can be more comfortable and less intimidating for children with sensory sensitivities. Choose one with a comfortable seat and a stable base.

### Introduce Gradual Desensitization:

Gradually expose the child to the different sensations associated with potty time. Start with short sessions and gradually increase the time spent in the bathroom. This can help desensitize the child to the sensory experiences over time.

### Offer Sensory-Friendly Wipes:

If using wipes, choose sensory-friendly options. Some children may prefer flushable wipes with different textures or scents. Allow the child to explore and choose the type of wipes they find comfortable.

### Use Visual Supports:

Visual schedules and supports can help children understand the sequence of events during potty time. Use visual aids, such as social stories or visual schedules, to prepare the child for what to expect.

### Provide Noise Reduction:

Some children may be sensitive to loud noises, such as flushing toilets. Consider using noise-reducing devices or closing the bathroom door to minimize auditory stimuli.

### Dress for Comfort:

Choose clothing that is comfortable and does not contribute to sensory discomfort. Avoid tight or scratchy clothing that may irritate. Some kids love being naked when going potty; if that is what they like at first and it makes them more comfortable, I say go for it!

### Use a Timer for Transition:

If transitions are challenging, you can use a visual timer to indicate the time spent in the bathroom. This can help the child anticipate when the potty time will end.

### Communicate Openly:

Encourage open communication with the child about their sensory preferences. Ask them about what makes them comfortable or uncomfortable during potty time, and adjust the environment accordingly.

Remember that each child is unique, so observing and understanding their individual sensory needs is important. Tailor the strategies to meet the specific preferences and sensitivities of the child and be flexible in adapting the approach as needed. Consistent positive reinforcement and a supportive environment can provide a more positive potty training experience for children with sensory sensitivities.

# Strategies for overcoming resistance

Overcoming resistance during potty training with autistic children requires a patient, understanding, and flexible approach. It's essential to identify and address the specific triggers causing resistance. This might involve sensory sensitivities, fear of change, or challenges in communication. Creating a visual schedule or social story tailored to the child's preferences can help make the process more predictable and reduce anxiety. Introduce the child to the bathroom gradually, allowing them to explore and become familiar with the environment. Be attuned to their sensory needs, such as adjusting lighting or providing comfort items like a favorite toy. Offer choices whenever possible to provide a sense of control, whether selecting a preferred toilet paper or choosing a reward for successful toileting. Consistency in routines, positive reinforcement, and celebrating small victories are key components in overcoming resistance. Recognizing that setbacks may occur is crucial, and maintaining a supportive, non-judgmental attitude is essential. Collaborating with the child's preferences and incorporating play or preferred activities during potty time can also turn resistance into a more engaging and positive experience, fostering a successful transition into independent toileting.

Overcoming resistance to using the bathroom in autistic children can be a gradual process that involves patience, understanding, and individualized strategies. Here are some strategies to help address resistance and facilitate a positive experience during potty training:

### Modify the Environment:

Address sensory sensitivities that may cause resistance. This could mean using a potty chair instead of a standard toilet to address fears of falling in, installing a dimmer switch or using a battery-operated candle for softer lighting, or providing a stool for stability. Making the bathroom a comfortable place for your child can significantly reduce resistance. Introduce a comfortable and child-friendly potty chair. Some children may find the regular toilet intimidating, and a potty chair can provide a more approachable and comfortable option.

### Practice Dry Runs:

When there's resistance to actually using the toilet, dry runs can be helpful. These are practice sessions where the child sits on the potty clothed to become comfortable with the idea without the pressure of needing to use it. Gradually, as comfort increases, encourage sitting on the potty without a diaper.

### Create a Predictable Routine:

Establish a consistent and predictable bathroom routine. Use visual schedules or social stories to help the child understand and anticipate the steps involved in using the bathroom. Consistency provides a sense of security and reduces anxiety.

## Offer Rewards and Positive Reinforcement:

Positive reinforcement is a powerful tool. Use a reward system that is meaningful to your child, such as stickers, extra playtime, or a small treat for successful potty attempts. Ensure the rewards are immediate and consistent to reinforce the desired behavior effectively.

## Provide Choices:

Offer the child choices to provide a sense of control and autonomy. Allow them to choose between different types of toilet paper, soap, or even the time they want to go to the bathroom within a reasonable schedule.

## Incorporate Special Interests:

Leverage your child's special interests to make potty training more engaging. Whether it's a favorite character on underwear or a storybook about potty training featuring beloved characters, integrating these interests can make the child more enthusiastic about participating in the process.

## Use Visual Aids:

Visual aids can be incredibly effective in guiding autistic children through the potty training process. Create a step-by-step visual guide of the potty routine and place it in the bathroom where your child can easily refer to it. This can help demystify the process and reduce anxiety about what is expected.

## Use Preferred Reinforcers:

Tailor the reinforcement to the child's preferences. Identify what motivates them the most and incorporate those preferences into the reinforcement system. This could include their favorite toys, activities, or snacks.

## Communicate Clearly and Calmly

Use simple, clear language to talk about potty training. For non-verbal or minimally verbal children, consider using sign language or picture exchange communication systems (PECS) to communicate about potty training needs.

### Include Preferred Activities:

Associate bathroom time with preferred activities. Allow the child to engage in a preferred activity immediately after using the bathroom successfully. This positive association can motivate them to cooperate.

### Be Patient and Flexible:

Remember, every child is different, and what works for one may not work for another. Be prepared to try different strategies and adjust your approach based on your child's response. Patience and flexibility are key.

### Collaborate with Professionals:

Consult with professionals, such as behavior analysts, occupational therapists, or speech therapists, who specialize in working with autistic children. They can provide additional insights, strategies, and support tailored to the child's individual needs.

Overcoming resistance to potty training in autistic children requires a thoughtful, personalized approach that respects their individual needs and challenges. By employing strategies that provide structure, address sensory issues, and use positive reinforcement, parents can create a supportive environment that encourages success. Remember, progress may be slow, and there will be setbacks, but with persistence, understanding, and the right strategies, potty training success is within reach. Celebrate the small victories along the way, and know that each step forward is a significant achievement for your child.

# Strategies for Encouraging Autistic Children to Use the Toilet for Pooping

Pooping in the toilet is a significant milestone for any child, but for those on the autism spectrum, it can present unique challenges. Sensory sensitivities, difficulty understanding bodily signals, routines, and the anxiety of new experiences can all play a role in making this aspect of potty training more complex. However, with thoughtful strategies and patience, parents and caregivers can support their autistic children in achieving success. Here are a few strategies for making pooping in the toilet a successful experience for autistic children.

## Understanding the Challenges

Before diving into strategies, it's crucial to acknowledge the specific challenges autistic children might face with pooping in the toilet. These can include:

- **Sensory Sensitivities:** Discomfort with the bathroom environment or the sensation of sitting on a toilet.
- **Routine and Change Resistance:** Difficulty in altering established routines, such as moving from diapers to using the toilet.
- **Communication Barriers**: Challenges in expressing needs or understanding instructions related to potty training.
- **Anxiety:** Fear of the unknown or the process itself, including the sound of flushing.

# Strategies for Success

### 1. Preparation and Familiarization

Start by familiarizing your child with the bathroom environment and the concept of using the toilet for pooping. You can read books or watch videos together that positively depict the process. Spend time in the bathroom without the pressure of having to use the toilet, just to explore and become comfortable with the space.

### 2. Create a Routine

Autistic children often respond well to routines. Establish a consistent bathroom schedule, particularly after meals, to take advantage of the body's natural timing. Use visual schedules or timers to signal when it's time to try sitting on the toilet. Your child will normally poop around the same time everyday. Establish that time frame and create a routine around it.

### 3. Use Visual Supports

Visual aids can help explain the process in a clear, sequential manner. Consider creating a visual storyboard that outlines the steps for using the toilet for pooping, such as "feel the need," "go to the bathroom," "sit on the toilet," and "wipe."

### 4. Address Sensory Issues

If sensory sensitivities are a significant barrier, try to make the bathroom as comfortable as possible. This might involve using a potty chair instead of a standard toilet, playing calming music, or adjusting the lighting.

Consider what specific sensory issues your child has and adapt the environment accordingly.

### 5. Encourage Sit and Wait

Encourage your child to sit on the toilet at regular intervals without the pressure to actually poop. This can help build comfort and familiarity with the sensation of sitting on the toilet. Reading a favorite book or playing with a small toy during this time can make the experience more pleasant.

### 6. Positive Reinforcement

Utilize a reward system for any progress made, not just for successfully pooping in the toilet. Rewards should be immediate, motivating, and specific to your child's interests. Positive verbal reinforcement and physical affection (if your child is receptive to it) can also be powerful motivators.

### 7. Model Behavior

If appropriate, model the behavior for your child. Children often learn through imitation, and seeing a parent or sibling use the toilet can demystify the process. You can also model where the poop goes, by taking it from their diaper/pull up, putting it into the toilet and flushing so they can visually see that is where it belongs.

### 8. Communication Tools

For non-verbal or minimally verbal children, provide tools to help them communicate their needs. This could be in the form of picture cards, signs, or digital apps designed for communication.

### 9. Patience and Flexibility

Progress may be slow, and there will likely be setbacks. It's important to remain patient and flexible, adjusting strategies as needed based on what works best for your child.

### 10. Seek Professional Guidance

If you encounter persistent difficulties, don't hesitate to seek support from professionals who specialize in autism and toilet training. They can provide personalized strategies and support tailored to your child's needs.

If you encounter persistent difficulties, don't hesitate to seek support from professionals who specialize in autism and toilet training. They can provide personalized strategies and support tailored to your child's needs.

The key ingredients for potty training success with pooping encompass a combination of understanding, patience, consistency, and positive reinforcement. Establishing a supportive environment tailored to your child's needs is essential, addressing any sensory sensitivities or anxieties surrounding the process. Consistency in routine and approach helps build predictability and confidence for your child, while clear communication and visual aids aid in understanding and motivation. Celebrating each step forward, no matter how small, with praise and rewards reinforces positive behavior and fosters a sense of accomplishment. Flexibility and resilience are also vital, as setbacks are a natural part of the learning process. With these ingredients in place, parents can navigate the challenges of potty training with pooping and support their child in achieving success and independence in this important milestone.

Successfully pooping in the toilet is a process that can vary greatly from one autistic child to another. By understanding the unique challenges your child faces and implementing strategies that cater to their needs, you can create a supportive and effective toilet training experience. Remember, every small step forward is an achievement worth celebrating. With patience, understanding, and the right approach, pooping in the toilet can become a comfortable and routine part of your child's life.

# Common Issues with Bowel Movements

Autism-related constipation can present significant challenges for autistic children, affecting their physical health, behavior, and overall well-being. One of the primary issues is sensory sensitivities, which can lead to aversion to certain textures or discomfort with the sensation of bowel movements. This aversion may result in withholding bowel movements, as children may actively resist the urge to go to the bathroom due to sensory discomfort or anxiety. Additionally, communication difficulties commonly observed in autistic children can make it challenging for them to express their discomfort or communicate their need to use the bathroom, further exacerbating the issue. As a result, constipation can become chronic, leading to abdominal pain, bloating, irritability, and changes in behavior.

Furthermore, the tendency to withhold bowel movements can create a vicious cycle, as the stool becomes harder and more difficult to pass, leading to increased discomfort and further resistance to bowel movements. This cycle can perpetuate constipation and exacerbate the problem over time. In addition to the physical discomfort, chronic constipation can have significant implications for a child's behavior and quality of life, impacting their ability to participate in daily activities, concentrate in school, and engage in social interactions. It is essential for parents, caregivers, and healthcare professionals to be aware of the challenges autistic children face when it comes to constipation and withholding bowel movements, and to implement strategies to support their physical and emotional well-being.

Gut health plays a crucial role in the overall well-being of autistic children, as emerging research suggests a strong connection between the gut and the brain, known as the gut-brain axis. Many autistic children experience gastrointestinal issues, including constipation, diarrhea, and abdominal pain, at higher rates than neurotypical children. These gastrointestinal symptoms may be linked to alterations in the gut microbiome, the community of microorganisms that inhabit the digestive tract, which can influence immune function, digestion, and even behavior and cognition. Addressing gut health in autistic children through dietary modifications, probiotics, and other interventions may not only alleviate gastrointestinal symptoms but also improve behavior, mood, and cognitive function. As our understanding of the gut-brain axis continues to evolve, prioritizing gut health in autistic children is increasingly recognized as an important aspect of holistic care and management.

# The Challenges of Autism-Related Constipation:

Autistic children may experience constipation due to a variety of factors, including:

- **Sensory Sensitivities**: Sensory issues can make it uncomfortable for children to use the bathroom or tolerate certain textures of food, leading to dietary choices that contribute to constipation.
- **Communication Difficulties:** Limited verbal communication skills can make it challenging for children to express their discomfort or communicate their need to use the bathroom.
- **Behavioral Patterns:** Some autistic children may develop patterns of withholding bowel movements as a coping mechanism for dealing with anxiety or sensory discomfort, leading to chronic constipation.

# Understanding Withholding Behavior:

Withholding bowel movements is a common issue among autistic children, and it can be a complex behavior rooted in various factors:

- **Sensory Discomfort**: Sensory sensitivities may make the sensation of having a bowel movement uncomfortable or overwhelming for some autistic children.
- **Anxiety and Control**: Fear or anxiety about using the bathroom, particularly in unfamiliar or public settings, can lead to a desire to control bowel movements by withholding.
- **Rigid Routine**: Autistic children often thrive on routine, and any disruption to their routine, such as changes in diet or environment, can trigger withholding behavior as a way to regain a sense of control.

# Strategies for Supporting Digestive Health:

### Dietary Modifications:

Ensure your child's diet includes plenty of fiber-rich foods, such as fruits, vegetables, whole grains, and legumes, to promote regular bowel movements. Be mindful of any sensory aversions to certain textures or tastes and offer alternatives. Also, natural supplements like probiotics can help with guy health. Be sure to consult with your child's pediatrician before giving hime or her any supplements.

### Hydration:

Encourage your child to drink plenty of water throughout the day to stay hydrated and support healthy digestion.

### Regular Bathroom Schedule:

Establish a consistent bathroom routine, including scheduled bathroom breaks after meals and before bedtime, to help regulate bowel movements and reduce withholding behavior.

### Sensory-Friendly Bathroom Environment:

Make the bathroom a comfortable and inviting space for your child by addressing any sensory sensitivities. Consider using soft lighting, playing calming music, or providing supportive seating options.

### Visual Supports:

Use visual schedules, social stories, or picture charts to help your child understand the bathroom routine and communicate their needs effectively.

### Positive Reinforcement:

Celebrate every successful bowel movement with praise and rewards to motivate and encourage your child. Focus on the process rather than the outcome to reinforce healthy habits.

### Consultation with Healthcare Professionals:

If constipation and withholding behavior persist despite your efforts, consult with your child's healthcare provider or a pediatric gastroenterologist for further evaluation and guidance.

Autism-related constipation and withholding behavior can pose significant challenges for both children and parents, but with understanding, patience, and effective strategies, it is possible to support your child's digestive health and overall well-being. By addressing sensory sensitivities, promoting healthy habits, and seeking professional guidance when needed, parents can empower their autistic children to achieve optimal digestive function and improve their quality of life. Remember that each child is unique, so be patient and flexible in finding the strategies that work best for your child.

# POTTY TRAINING ON THE GO: Public Restrooms and Travel

Potty training can be a challenging milestone for any child, but for autistic children, who may have unique sensory sensitivities, communication barriers, and a preference for routine, it can require additional patience and tailored strategies. When it comes to potty training on the go, using public restrooms, and managing travel, these challenges can be amplified. Here are some approaches and tips that may help:

## Before Starting:

| | |
|---|---|
| **Preparation is Key:** | Before embarking on any trip, prepare your child by explaining what to expect using simple, clear language or visual aids. Social stories about using public restrooms can be particularly helpful. |
| **Familiarize Through Play:** | Use playtime to familiarize your child with the concept of using a potty away from home. There are toy toilets, and you can role-play with dolls or action figures. |
| **Sensory Sensitivities:** | Be mindful of sensory issues. The loud flush of a public toilet or the feel of different toilet seats can be distressing. Practice at home with noise-cancelling headphones or carry a portable seat cover to make unfamiliar toilets less daunting. |

# Potty Training on the Go

| | |
|---|---|
| **Portable Potty:** | Consider bringing a portable potty or seat reducer for your child. This can offer a consistent and familiar option no matter where you are. |
| **Routine and Scheduling:** | Try to maintain a routine even when out. If your child is used to going to the toilet at certain times, aim to stick to these times as closely as possible. |
| **Cue Cards and Communication Devices:** | If your child uses any communication aids, ensure they have the means to signal the need to use the bathroom while out. Cue cards with symbols or pictures can be handy. |

# In Public Restrooms

| | |
|---|---|
| **Scout Ahead:** | Look for family or accessible restrooms that offer more space and privacy. Check them out before bringing your child in to ensure they're clean and quiet if possible. |
| **Practice Runs:** | If feasible, visit public restrooms in less busy times to get your child accustomed to them without the pressure of urgency. |
| **Handy Kit:** | Carry a kit including wipes, hand sanitizer, disposable seat covers, and a change of clothes. This can help manage cleanliness concerns and accidents more smoothly. |
| **Distraction and Comfort:** | Have a small toy, book, or device that can distract or soothe your child if they are feeling overwhelmed by the sensory environment. |

## When Traveling

| | |
|---|---|
| **Accommodation Considerations:** | When booking accommodations, consider options with kitchenette facilities. Having a private bathroom with more control over the environment can be very helpful. |
| **Travel Potty:** | For longer trips, especially by car, a travel potty is invaluable. It allows for quick stops and ensures that a familiar potty is always available. |
| **Itinerary Planning:** | Plan your itinerary with regular bathroom breaks and know where restrooms are located at your destinations. |
| **Comfort Items:** | Bring along any comfort items or familiar objects that help your child feel secure and calm. |

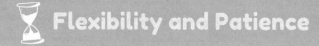

## Flexibility and Patience

Above all, flexibility and patience are crucial. Every child is different, and what works for one may not work for another. Be prepared to try different strategies and to possibly face setbacks. Celebrate small victories and remain positive and supportive.

## Seeking Support

Remember, it's okay to seek support. Connecting with other parents of autistic children through forums, support groups, or social media can provide valuable insights and encouragement. Additionally, professionals such as occupational therapists who specialize in sensory issues can offer guidance tailored to your child's needs.

Potty training while on the go presents unique challenges, but with preparation, adaptation, and support, you can help your child achieve this important milestone.

# CHAPTER 7
# PROGRESS MONITORING AND ADJUSTMENTS

Tracking milestones and setbacks during potty training is crucial for understanding the child's progress and making informed adjustments to the training plan. Here are steps you can take to track milestones and setbacks effectively:

## 1. Establish Clear Goals:

Define specific and achievable goals for potty training. These goals could include using the toilet independently, communicating bathroom needs, or washing hands afterward. Make sure the goals are realistic and tailored to the child's abilities.

## 2. Create a Potty Training Chart:

Use a potty training chart to visually track milestones. Include columns for date, time, and specific behaviors or actions related to potty training. This provides a quick and easy way to monitor progress over time. I have created a data sheet you can use to track your child's progress on a daily basis. This gives you an idea of your child's success and what they might need to work on.

## 3. Record Daily Observations:

Keep a daily log or journal where you record observations related to potty training. Note the times when the child successfully uses the toilet, any communication efforts, and instances of setbacks or challenges.

## 4. Maintain Communication with Professionals:

Regularly communicate with professionals, such as behavioral therapists or occupational therapists. Share tracking data, observations, and concerns to receive guidance and insights into refining the potty training plan.

### 5. Document Setbacks and Challenges:

Record instances of setbacks or challenges as well. Documenting these moments is essential for understanding what might trigger setbacks and how to address them. Note changes in routine, environment, or other factors that may contribute to challenges

### 6. Identify Patterns:

Review the tracking data regularly to identify patterns or trends. Look for consistent times of success, common challenges, or any factors that influence the child's behavior during potty training.

### 7. Adjust Strategies Based on Data:

Use the information gathered to adjust and refine potty training strategies. If certain approaches seem particularly effective, consider reinforcing them. Likewise, if setbacks are noted, explore alternative strategies or seek professional advice.

### 8. Set Realistic Expectations:

Set realistic expectations for the pace of progress. Understand that setbacks are a natural part of the process, and progress may be gradual. Adjust goals and expectations accordingly.

### 9. Review and Reflect:

Periodically review the tracking data and reflect on the overall progress. Consider what has been effective, what needs adjustment, and how the child's needs may have evolved during the potty training process.

By consistently tracking milestones and setbacks, you can gain valuable insights into the child's potty training journey. This information helps create a more informed, individualized approach that maximizes success and minimizes challenges.

# Modifying strategies as needed:

Modifying strategies that aren't working is an essential aspect of supporting autistic children through various challenges, including potty training. Here's a guide on how you can adapt and adjust your child's approach when faced with obstacles:

### 1. IDENTIFY THE SPECIFIC CHALLENGE

Start by pinpointing the specific aspect of the strategy that isn't working. Is it the timing, the environment, the communication method, or the type of reinforcement? Understanding the root cause of the difficulty will guide your modifications effectively.

### 2. ASSESS YOUR CHILD'S NEEDS

Consider your child's unique sensory sensitivities, communication style, and preferences. What works well for one child may not work for another. Tailor your modifications to align with your child's individual needs and strengths.

### 3. EXPLORE ALTERNATIVE APPROACHES

Research and explore alternative strategies or methods that may better suit your child's needs. This could involve trying different types of visual supports, communication tools, or reinforcement techniques. Be open-minded and willing to experiment to find what works best.

## 4. INVOLVE YOUR CHILD IN THE PROCESS

Solicit your child's input and involvement in finding solutions. They may have insights into what is causing difficulties or ideas for adjustments that could make the strategy more effective for them. Collaborating with your child empowers them and promotes self-awareness and problem-solving skills.

## 5. MAKE INCREMENTAL CHANGES

Avoid making drastic changes all at once, as this can be overwhelming for both you and your child. Instead, make small, incremental adjustments to the strategy and observe how your child responds. Gradually fine-tune the approach based on their feedback and progress.

## 6. STAY CONSISTENT WITH ROUTINES

While making modifications, maintain consistency with other aspects of your child's routine, such as timing and reinforcement. Consistency provides a sense of predictability and stability for your child, which is especially important for autistic children.

## 7. MONITOR AND EVALUATE PROGRESS

Continuously monitor your child's progress and evaluate the effectiveness of the modified strategies. Keep track of what is working well and what still needs improvement. Regularly reassess and make further adjustments as needed.

### 8. SEEK PROFESSIONAL GUIDANCE

Don't hesitate to seek guidance from professionals, such as therapists or behavioral specialists, who have experience working with autistic children. They can offer valuable insights, suggestions, and support tailored to your child's specific needs.

### 9. STAY PATIENT AND PERSISTENT

Rome wasn't built in a day, and neither is progress in potty training or any other developmental milestone. Stay patient and persistent, recognizing that setbacks are a normal part of the learning process. Celebrate every small success along the way.

### 10. TAKE CARE OF YOURSELF

Lastly, remember to prioritize self-care. Supporting an autistic child through challenges can be emotionally and physically demanding. Take breaks when needed, seek support from friends and family, and don't hesitate to ask for help when necessary.

By following these steps and being proactive in modifying strategies that aren't working, you can effectively support your autistic child through the potty training journey and other developmental milestones, fostering a positive and empowering learning environment.

# CHAPTER 8
# TRANSITIONING TO INDEPENDENCE

# Gradual steps toward independent toileting:

Transitioning to independence in potty training is a gradual process that involves empowering the child to take on more responsibilities and fostering self-care skills. Here are steps to help facilitate the transition to independence in potty training:

### Establish a Solid Foundation:

Ensure that your child has a solid foundation in basic toileting routines. This includes understanding the purpose of using the toilet, recognizing the sensation of needing to go, and following a consistent toileting schedule.

### Introduce Independence Gradually:

Gradually introduce independence by allowing your child to take on more toileting-related tasks. Start with simple steps, such as pulling down pants or using the flush, and progressively add more responsibilities as your child becomes comfortable.

### Encourage Self-Initiation:

Encourage your child to self-initiate bathroom breaks. Teach them to recognize the cues that indicate the need to use the toilet and empower them to express when they need to go independently.

### Teach Wiping Skills:

Teach and practice wiping skills. Provide guidance on proper techniques, and gradually allow your child to take on this task with increasing independence. Consider using flushable wipes for added convenience.

### Promote Handwashing Independence:

Encourage handwashing independence. Teach your child proper handwashing techniques and provide any necessary support until they can complete the task independently.

### Use Visual Supports:

Use visual supports, such as visual schedules or checklists, to guide your child through independent toileting. Visual aids help reinforce the sequence of actions and promote a sense of predictability.

### Establish a Signal for Bathroom Needs:

If not already in place, establish a clear signal or communication method for your child to express their need to use the toilet independently. This could be a specific gesture, a verbal cue, or a visual symbol.

### Transition to Regular Underwear:

Gradually transition from pull-ups or training pants to regular underwear. This step reinforces the expectation of staying dry and encourages your child to be more aware of their body's signals.

### Celebrate Independence:

Celebrate and praise your child for every successful attempt at independent toileting. Positive reinforcement fosters a sense of accomplishment and motivation for continued efforts.

### Set Up a Step Stool:

Place a step stool near the toilet to help your child reach the sink and toilet more easily. This promotes independence in tasks such as washing hands and getting on and off the toilet.

### Encourage Dressing Independence:

Encourage dressing and undressing independence. Choose easy clothing for your child to manage, and provide guidance on pulling down and pulling up pants independently.

### Establish Consistency Across Environments:

Ensure consistency in independent toileting across different environments, such as home, school, and other places your child visits often. Coordination with caregivers and educators is key.

### Use a Reward System:

Implement a reward system that reinforces independent toileting. Consider using a reward chart where your child earns stickers or tokens for each successful independent toileting task, leading to a larger reward after a certain number of stickers.

### Monitor and Adjust:

Continuously monitor your child's progress and be ready to adjust your approach based on their needs. If certain aspects of independence are challenging, seek input from professionals or consider modifying strategies.

### Encourage Open Communication:

Foster open communication about your child's feelings and experiences during the transition. Encourage them to express any concerns or discomfort and address these in a supportive manner.

The transition to independence in using the potty is a crucial milestone for autistic children, holding immense importance for their overall development and well-being. Beyond the practical aspect of personal hygiene, mastering this skill fosters a sense of autonomy and self-confidence in the child, laying the groundwork for greater independence in various aspects of life. For autistic children, who may already face challenges in communication, sensory processing, and social interactions, achieving independence in using the potty represents a significant step towards overcoming barriers and navigating the world with greater ease. Moreover, mastering this skill enhances their participation in daily activities, promotes a sense of control over their bodies and environment, and reduces dependence on caregivers. Ultimately, empowering autistic children to become independent in using the potty not only enhances their quality of life but also promotes their overall development and integration into society.

# Fading prompts and support

## Introduce Choice and Control:

Provide opportunities for your child to make choices and control the task. This encourages them to take more initiative.

## Use Natural Reinforcement:

Shift from artificial reinforcement (prompting) to natural reinforcement for successful task completion. Allow the natural consequences of completing the task to serve as reinforcement.

## Encourage Self-Monitoring:

Encourage self-monitoring by teaching your child to assess their own performance. This includes recognizing errors, self-correction, and evaluating the need for assistance.

## Monitor for Generalization:

Assess the generalization of skills across different settings and situations. It's important that your child can perform the task independently in various environments, not just in the training context.

## Fade Across Settings and People:

Ensure that prompts are faded not only across different settings but also across different people providing support. The goal is for your child to demonstrate independence regardless of who is present.

## Celebrate Successes:

Celebrate your child's successes as they achieve greater independence. Positive reinforcement and acknowledgment of their efforts contribute to a positive learning experience.

Remember that the fading process should be tailored to your child's needs. Regularly assess progress, communicate openly, and be patient as you guide your child toward greater independence.

# CHAPTER 9
# COLLABORATION WITH CAREGIVERS AND PROFESSIONALS

# Involving parents, teachers, and therapists:

Collaborating with professionals during the potty training process for an autistic child is crucial for ensuring a comprehensive and effective approach. Here are steps you can take to foster collaboration with professionals:

### 1. BUILD A SUPPORT TEAM:

Identify and assemble a support team including pediatricians, behavioral therapists, occupational therapists, speech therapists, and educators. Ensure everyone is aware of the potty training goals and strategies.

### 2. SHARE INFORMATION:

Provide comprehensive information about the child's strengths, challenges, and individualized needs related to potty training. Share any relevant medical history, sensory sensitivities, or communication preferences.

### 3. ESTABLISH OPEN COMMUNICATION:

Foster open and regular communication with professionals involved in the child's care. Share updates on progress, setbacks, and any observations about the child's behavior during the potty training.

### 4. PARTICIPATE IN MEETINGS:

Meet with professionals to discuss the child's progress and address concerns. Collaborative meetings can involve parents, caregivers, teachers, therapists, and other individuals working closely with the child.

### 5. SEEK PROFESSIONAL GUIDANCE:

Consult with professionals for guidance on developing a customized potty training plan. Behavioral therapists, in particular, can provide strategies for addressing challenging behaviors and reinforcing positive ones.

### 6. IMPLEMENT CONSISTENT STRATEGIES:

Ensure that the strategies professionals recommend are implemented consistently across various environments, including home, school, and any other relevant settings. Consistency is crucial for generalizing skills.

### 7. PROVIDE REGULAR UPDATES:

Regularly update professionals on the child's progress and any changes in behavior or needs. This information helps them make informed adjustments to interventions and strategies.

### 8. INCORPORATE THERAPEUTIC TECHNIQUES:

If applicable, incorporate therapeutic techniques suggested by professionals. For example, occupational therapists may recommend specific sensory activities that can be integrated into the potty training routine.

### 9. ASK FOR DEMONSTRATIONS OR TRAINING:

Request demonstrations or training sessions from professionals, especially if some specific techniques or interventions need to be implemented during the potty training process. This hands-on guidance can be valuable.

### 10. SHARE OBSERVATIONS:

Share your observations of the child's responses to different strategies during potty training. Professionals can use this information to refine their recommendations and adjust as needed.

### 11. COLLABORATE ON GOAL SETTING:

Work collaboratively with professionals to set realistic and achievable potty training goals. These goals should be tailored to the child's abilities and developmental level.

### 12. ADVOCATE FOR THE CHILD:

Be an advocate for the child by communicating their needs, preferences, and progress. Professionals can better support the child when they thoroughly understand the individual's unique characteristics.

## 13. ATTEND WORKSHOPS OR TRAINING SESSIONS:

Attend workshops or training sessions offered by professionals or relevant organizations focusing on potty training strategies for children with autism. This can enhance your understanding of effective approaches.

## 14. BE OPEN TO FEEDBACK:

Be open to receiving feedback from professionals and be willing to adjust the potty training plan based on their expertise. Collaboration involves a two-way exchange of information and ideas.

Remember, collaboration is a dynamic process, and ongoing communication is key. Working with professionals can create a supportive and effective environment for the child during the potty training process.

# CHAPTER 10
# RESOURCES AND SUPPORT NETWORKS

# GOALLY! BEST TOOL!

**10% OFF**
Use our code **"LJ10"**

SCAN ME

# USEFUL APPS

Several tools and apps can be useful for potty training children with autism. These tools often incorporate visual supports, social stories, and interactive features to help make the potty training process more accessible and engaging. Here are some examples:

### 1. Potty Time with Elmo:

- Platform: iOS, Android
- Description: This app, featuring Sesame Street's Elmo, uses songs and videos to teach children about potty time. It includes a customizable potty chart and a timer to help with scheduled bathroom breaks.

### 2. Potty Whiz: Training App

- Platform: iOS
- Description: This app allows you to create customizable potty charts and provides a timer to help schedule regular bathroom breaks. It includes visual cues, rewards for successful toilet use, and a schedule to keep track of your child's progress.

### 3. Potty Toilet Training

- Platform: iOS
- Description: This app provides a timer to help schedule regular bathroom breaks for those scheduled trips. It includes reminders of potty time, and you can access the history activity of your child's potty training progress.

Before using any app or tool, assessing its suitability for the child's needs and preferences is essential. Additionally, consider involving parents, caregivers, and professionals in selecting and implementing these tools to ensure a coordinated and effective approach to potty training for children with autism.

**Here is a list of materials you will need to start your Potty Training Journey and make it a success!**

**Here is the Potty Training Social Story:**

**Here is the token board/ visual schedules:**

**Here is our online shop where you can purchase other resources:**

# References:

1. "What Are the three levels of Autism?" By: Nancy Lovering, https://psychcentral.com/autism/levels-of-autism#level-1 , 2022.

2. "The Potty Journey: Guide to Toilet Training Children with Special Needs, Including Autism and Related Disorders"  by: Judith A. Coucouvanis, 2008

3. Wheeler, Maria. "Toilet Training for Individuals with Autism or Other Developmental Issues". [Future Horizons], 2007.

4. Autism Speaks. "Toilet Training." *Autism Speaks*, https://www.autismparentingmagazine.com/autism-potty-training-guide/ , 2023.

5. "Potty Training and the Use of Positive Reinforcement" Bridget A. Taylor, Psy.D., Robert L. Koegel, Ph.D

Made in United States
Troutdale, OR
11/04/2024